EVANCE

Series Editor: MEIC STEPHENS

The Aesthetics of Relevance

Peter Lord

GOMER

First Impression — 1992

ISBN 0 86383 897 9

Printed in Wales by
J. D. Lewis and Sons Ltd., Gomer Press, Llandysul, Dyfed

'The first article of an Ascendancy's creed is, and always has been, that the natives are a lesser breed, and that anything that is theirs (except their land and their gold!) is therefore of little value . . . In the course of time the natives become tainted with these doctrines, and cry approval when the untruths of the Ascendancy are echoed from some distant place, as if at last a fair judgement has been pronounced . . .'

Daniel Corkery in *The Hidden Ireland* (1924)

I. A VISUAL HANDICAP

This is an essay about the present, even if it does pay a lot of attention to the past. The idea that the Welsh are unvisual is mainly a nineteenth-century construct but it remains one of the dominant assumptions of, and about, the people. It achieved its most explicit, public, and authoritative expression in the words I have often quoted from David Bell's book, *The Artist in Wales*, published in 1957: 'At no time since the Norman Conquest at any rate has the Welshman had any visual artistic tradition.' Let me make it clear once again that Bell failed—unwittingly or on purpose—to make a distinction of fundamental importance in understanding our culture. There is a difference between a tradition of art and works of art. The idea that Bell expressed was not that Wales had no tradition, but simply that Wales had no visual art, indeed no indigenous visual culture.

A tradition is a concept, not a collection of material. It is an intellectual structure into which—in this case—visual images are fitted. It is this structure, or simply this story, which activates the images in a culture. Without being activated in this way, by recognition and incorporation in a tradition, to all intents and purposes the images do not exist. The phenomenon of an unrecognized visual culture is not unusual in modern history, as we shall see.

A tradition links images together, and links them to the wider culture of which the makers and consumers of the images were a part. It also links them to the contemporary culture of the tradition-maker, so that in temporal terms a visual tradition is dualistic. Like all history, it is retrospective in that it deals with past events, linking them into an evolutionary process, but like all ideas it belongs first of all to the time in which it is made. It is the contemporaneity of a tradition that makes it an active and significant force in our lives. Unless the tradition is periodically reconstructed in ways appropriate to changed aspirations, the images it reveals are rendered irrelevant.

The idea that the Welsh are unvisual has been and continues to be damaging to the health of the culture. Even in this age of sensitivity to racism it still implies a sort of congenital deficiency in the people. As recently as 1987 the art historian Donald Moore felt it worth discussing this idea at an art symposium: 'It would seem that Welsh people notice mainly their friends', he observed, 'and that the surroundings melt into a kind of mist, as in the pictures of Beatrix Potter, which reflect the vision of a child. Is the indifference to visual experience a matter of inheritance or simply of arrested development?' [1]

The idea undermines the culture by telling us that Wales is incomplete. The notion of an incomplete—and consequently inadequate—national culture, as presented in Wales by Anglocentric art historians, is a powerful constraint on political evolution. No culture functions without a complex visual language, and so, in the absence of an indigenous tradition, the visual tradition of a competing culture is introduced to fill the vacuum. The result is a mis-match between the borrowed visual culture and the complex of understandings which inform the established elements of national tradition through literature.

Cultural incoherence of this kind and the lack of confidence manifested by people in such situations inhibit the development of new imagery characteristic of the indigenous culture complex. Image-makers in Wales are familiar with only a small vocabulary of resonant images on which to build, and when they do attempt to make work with national implications they find it hard to get taken seriously, in a way in which English artists do not. Our lack of confidence disables us from taking our own product as seriously as we take the product of other cultures, both as makers and as consumers. The visual image is an essential medium for the assertion of national identity: the denial of the aesthetics of the one is the denial of the politics of the other.

[1] *Art in a Small Nation,* pub. Welsh Arts Council and University College of Wales, Aberystwyth, 1987, p.87.

II. THE HISTORY OF A NATIONAL PHOBIA

In the seventeenth and early eighteenth centuries the only perceptions of nationality of which we can speak with any certainty are the perceptions of the gentry and of intellectuals. English and Welsh perceptions of Wales at this time were closely linked together. The English, into the early eighteenth century, regarded Wales, and the Welsh in Wales, as barbarous, having no arts of any kind. Naturally enough, the Welsh gentry did not regard themselves as barbarous but would certainly have agreed that their civilzation depended upon their familiarity with English manners and tastes. In English society, being Welsh was something of a social handicap by association with this perception of barbarity. It did not exclude personal progress in the arts, but required physical transfer to London, linguistic transfer to English, and activity within the framework of English institutions and conventions. These conventions were shared by Welsh patrons and exemplified by the great baroque memorials of the Wynn and Myddleton families executed by Robert Wynne before 1720, for instance. Welsh sculptors such as Wynne, and painters such as Edward Owen, trained in a perfectly satisfactory way in early eighteenth-century London without, as far as one can tell, being regarded as in any way exceptional.

Around the middle of the eighteenth century there occurred the well-documented change of perceptions which transformed Welshness from a social handicap into a desirable social asset in England. However, there were no immediate implications for modern Welsh culture in Wales itself. The country was perceived as a kind of relic, and essentially what happened was that relics became fashionable.

The Tudor construct of an ancient British ancestry legitimizing English domination of the islands of Britain was energetically developed, and the living Welsh—by their also being in some obscure way related to this heritage—achieved a new respectability. The consequent confidence facilitated the reconstruction of a literary tradition ambiguously feeding both a sense of Welsh separateness and strengthening the legitimacy of English hegemony. Nevertheless, this tradition was in general terms perceived by Welsh and English alike as a sort of living archaeology, and certainly not as art. It was neither of the same kind nor of equal status to contemporary English art, which continued to develop on its classical base.

For instance, Thomas Pennant felt able to be unreservedly patriotic in his *Tours in Wales,* published in 1778 and 1781. He talked of 'our literature' and opened his description with the resounding 'I now speak of my native country . . .'. On the other hand, Pennant did not extrapolate from the literary (and indeed political) tradition he described to an expectation that there ought to be a modern indigenous art culture in Wales. For Pennant, the contemporary expression of the Welsh identity he so confidently asserted was in English culture. He could now feel that that culture included him. Ancient British history had reappeared in English poetry and painting as a symbol of freedom and the Romantic soul.

The assessment of the quality of indigenous Welsh culture did not arise, therefore. One does not generally question the aesthetics of relics: they are valued because of their age. The virtual absence of art institutions and academic painters and sculptors based in Wales was not perceived by Pennant as a Welsh shortcoming because he had no reason to expect to find them here. More than that, they were to be found in London in the van of avant-garde English culture as individuals, and also grouped together in the first national institution of Wales, the Cymmrodorion Society. In the visual arts in particular Pennant could easily have confirmed the rectitude of his world-view, had he ever doubted it. Although Richard Wilson's career was in decline by the time the *Tours* reached the press, for over thirty years he had been a leading light in the English art world, a founder member of the Royal Academy. At the same time Watkin Williams Wynn, second president of the Cymmrodorion, was numbered among the great visual art patrons of all Europe. Both these men were conspicuously Welsh, in the same way as Pennant. He himself, by his patronage of Moses Griffith, had shown that the Welsh of humble origins were as capable of rising in the visual arts as those of gentry lineage like Wilson.

However, the reconstruction of the political history and literary tradition of Wales was accompanied by the discovery and re-evaluation of Wales the place by the English, and consequently its re-evaluation by the Welsh too. Pennant was an important influence in this process, of course. Travel, written descriptions, and above all visual images, required that the foundation myth be related to a contemporary physical reality. This made the concept of the smooth continuum from ancient British into modern English culture, enthusiastically espoused by Gray,[2] somewhat less than straightforward for younger Welsh intellectuals. The idea of a contemporary Welsh nation with certain distinguishing characteristics, as a parallel entity to England, began to suggest itself in a muddled sort of way in their minds. They began to make assessments of the quality of the contemporary culture and suggestions as to its improvement.

Edward Pugh, the painter and writer, presented readers of his *Cambria Depicta* with many such assessments: 'When in the neighbourhood of any good houses, I made it my business to inquire, and get all the information I could, about collections of paintings, and where it was probable that there were any good pictures; but I was continually disappointed. Indeed a general apathy and want of taste for the arts, and I may add for the sciences, are too observable among my countrymen; which may account why so few natives excel in them. Talents, in a latent state, may exist among them; but while these are to encounter all the discouragement of neglect, and no fostering hand to appear to cherish and hold forth the means of purchasing the bent of genius, they are left like

> "Many a flower, born to blush unseen,
> And waste its sweetness in the desert air".'

Pugh's comparisons were usually, though not always, unfavourable. He was an émigré intellectual in London, and this experience provided him with a prestigious model which inevitably found Welsh culture wanting. Wales simply was not England. However, the expectation that it might be, implicit in the comparison, was a considerable development of national consciousness over Pennant. Indeed, Pugh's consciousness was

[2] See Peter Lord, 'Y Bardd—Celtiaeth a Chelfyddyd', *Cof Cenedl,* 1992.

sufficiently advanced to suggest an institutional remedy: 'The superfluous wealth of the country is fully competent to form and sustain a national work, or some institution that might be the means of thus cherishing the buds of native genius, and of giving energy to more matured talents, which may sometimes be found even among the wilds of Penmachno and the Vales of Nantglyn.'

Pugh's English model suggested to him that there ought to have been an identifiably Welsh art-world—a system of institutional and private patronage, of teaching and of critical assessment.[3] As he was writing, his contemporaries in London were commissioning and making the first explicitly national art of modern Wales. Pieces such as the Raimbach 'Hu Gadarn' mark the beginning of Wales seeing, rather than simply being seen. In *Cambria Depicta* Edward Pugh responded enthusiastically to much the most famous of these commissions, Philippe de Loutherbourg's 'Bard' for Edward Jones' *Musical and Poetical Relicks of the Welsh Bards*.

The development of national consciousness represented by Pugh's work compared to Pennant's also found expression in the expectation that Wales, as a complete nation, should manifest a modern music culture. When the *Eisteddfodau Taleithiol* were established at Carmarthen in 1819 the only significant controversy that arose concerned the inclusion of modern art music in the activities. The energy of the young John Jones. (Bardd Alaw) was directed not only towards the maintenance of the relics of indigenous music, but also towards demonstrating the ability of the Welsh intellectual community to sustain a modern art culture on the model of English taste—in particular the taste for Italian opera. This aspiration put him at odds with an older generation of Pennant-like antiquarians, represented in music in particular by John Jenkins (Ifor Ceri) who saw no need for modern music in a Welsh festival which was, by definition, a festival of living archaeology. This resulted later in his memorable accusation that Bardd Alaw had turned the Eisteddfod into 'an Anglo-Italian farce'.

[3] Edward Pugh was also conscious of the example of Scotland; 'We frequently hear of the nationality of the Scotch, than whom no people seem to have a warmer friendship for each other; an example worthy of the imitation of all countries, and particularly of Wales . . .' *Cambria Depicta*, p.76

The grafting of modern art music onto nineteenth-century Welsh culture was of course a resounding success so that within half a century the tradition of '*Cymru Lân, Gwlad y Gân*' had been invented, and no patriot to this day, even when attacking the expenditure of millions of pounds on Welsh National Opera, goes out of his or her way to declare that the Welsh are *not* a musical nation.[4] Public patronage continues to elaborate this construct with its 'Singer of the World' competition and other Tourist Board jamborees. Visual art proved not nearly so tractible a problem, but the attempt to graft it on was made at the same time, and by the same people, and by very much the same means, and it should be remembered that this attempt was made with a much more prestigious base in modern culture on which to build in the persons of Wilson, and in the first half of the nineteenth century, John Gibson.

The painter Hugh Hughes, in association with the Cymmrodorion, made a short-lived attempt at establishing a national portrait gallery in 1830, but the Eisteddfod movement, first at Abergavenny in the 1840s, and then through the reformed National Eisteddfod in the 1860s, provided the main focus for attempts to develop modern art culture in Wales. Professional academic artists and art-oriented intellectuals—and there were numbers of both in this period, nearly all based in London—organized exhibitions and competitions, and invested time and money in the speculative creation of national art, in particular of sculpture. 'Who have made themselves more famous than the Welsh in the fields of art and science!', remarked one 'Philos' in 1866. 'But why must they go away from home to win fame and status? Because there are no institutions in Wales which recognize and sympathize with the talent given into their keeping. Let the Eisteddfod from now on value and reward its sons for meritorious productions of all kinds. In this way we will grow in respect and honour, and homage will be paid to us by the enlightened nations of Christendom'.[5]

[4] See Hywel Teifi Edwards, 'Y Gân a Ganai Morlais' and other essays in *Codi'r Hen Wlad yn ei Hôl,* pub. Gomer, 1989.

[5] *Y Gwladgarwr,* 31 March, 1866.

The attempt to graft modern academic art onto nineteenth-century Welsh culture before about 1880 met with only the most limited success. The reason is not hard to find. The ephemeral nature of the Eisteddfod with its émigré intellectual base made it a quite inappropriate institution to develop a material culture. Further, it was working in a power-vacuum as there were no resident national institutions which could make use of the art produced and sponsor the production of more. Even the church was foreign. Only a tiny number of the pieces made in this context have survived.

Modern academic art was perceived as a proof of the quality of a culture, and so the implications of this failure were serious. After Edward Pugh we may say that the impression grew—as national consciousness grew—of a Welsh deficiency in the visual arts, and that this national deficiency was in some way congenital in the people. This suspicion was sustained by the increasingly strong identification of culture characteristics with race through the nineteenth and early twentieth century, and the general collapse of confidence in the indigenous culture following the publication of the Blue Books in 1847. By the 1880s the National Eisteddfod, rather than rectifying the perception, served more often than not to confirm it, although there were some notable exceptions in the form of large art and craft exhibitions in 1868, 1876 and 1883.

The year 1908 was a particularly bad one. At the Eisteddfod the painter (and patriot) Christopher Williams noted that 'there seems, somehow, to be no conception among the Welsh people of what art really is. Ninety-nine out of every hundred treat it with an indifference which suggests that they think it means only painting pretty pictures'. Meanwhile, Augustus John, who could hardly be described as a patriot, rehearsed from a safe distance in Paris all three of the commonly proposed explanations for the national visual handicap: 'In Wales, I am told, lies the hidden soul of art; the body being doubtless no less reticent and inconspicuous . . . Do the Welsh people want art? Do they even respect it? There is no people who need it [more], body and soul. It seems the Welsh prefer emotions to things; their neglected sense of beauty evaporates in fits of yawning after periodical attacks of spiritual insomnia; their architectural sense is exhausted in the effort to construct New Jerusalem; their sense of design just suffices to render intelligible to them the scheme of the universe;—while form, colour, suggest ideas entirely trivial or vaguely diabolical'.[6]

III. EXPLAINING THE VISUAL HANDICAP

a. PATRONAGE—'AN UNENTERPRISING PEOPLE'

Since the time of Edward Pugh some artists and writers about art have been in no doubt that the want of academic art in Wales has resulted from the want of patronage. Few have proceeded beyond that point to analyse the reasons for this apparent failure. The phenomenon has been left as an unexplained and essentially mysterious one, reinforcing the idea that it represents a congenital shortcoming of the people. *The Times* expressed this explicitly in an editorial of 1866 which reviewed the National Eisteddfod Art and Industrial Exhibition: 'Wales, it should be remembered, is a small country, unfavourably situated for commercial purposes, with an indifferent soil, and inhabited by an unenterprising people. A bare existence on the most primitive food of a mountainous race is all that the Welsh could enjoy if left to themselves. Under such circumstances what could be more out of place than an exhibition designed to foster satisfaction with Welsh productions and Welsh virtues? All the progress and civilisation in Wales has come from England, and a sensible Welshman would direct all his endeavours towards inducing his countrymen to appreciate their neighbours instead of themselves... The sooner all Welsh specialities disappear from the face of the earth the better'.

David Bell's version of this text nearly a century later was that 'If the artist in Wales is to make any distinction of nationality it must be to note how great is the debt of Wales to England and how tardy the Welsh have been to take advantage of their wealthier if not naturally more artistic neighbour'. One of Bell's

[6] *Wales Today and Tomorrow*, ed. T.Stephens, 1908.

early acolytes, Wyn Griffith, remarked, even more enthusiastically, in 1951, 'So much for the past. No patron, no critic, therefore no painter, no sculptor, no Welsh art. It is as simple as that'.[7] Such comments may not be taken lightly—Griffith was the Chairman of the Welsh Committee of the Arts Council of Great Britain at the time and Bell the Art Officer. As recently as 1985 a later follower, Eric Rowan, in his book *Art in Wales*, written for the Arts Council, noted his indebtedness to Bell's work for 'the attitude it adopts and the priorities it defines'. Rowan's use of patronising tone and pejorative adjectives, masquerading as an 'impersonal attitude', insinuated the same idea of a congenital deficiency in the context of his failure to analyse the processes of patronage. Having pronounced that in any case Welsh subject-matter was inadequate to sustain a category of art, he concluded by ridiculing a deliberately distorted and caricatured notion of what constitutes an indigenous visual culture by paraphrasing Jackson Pollock: 'The idea of an isolated Welsh painting seems absurd to me, just as the idea of creating a purely Welsh mathematics or physics would seem'.

In a more charitable, but equally condescending mood, David Bell had also sought to excuse the patronage failure in terms of poverty. 'A small peasant people like the Welsh', he remarked, 'does not, cannot provide the conditions in which the fine arts flourish or in which the crafts can be found on any but an elementary level... Had the Welsh had the same circumstances as a rich urban people they might have produced great painters or fine cities or handsome books or beautiful stained glass. These things might have founded a great tradition of the visual arts, but in fact they have not done so'.

As we have seen, Edward Pugh had pointed out 150 years earlier that poverty was not the cause. The wealth of Watkin Williams Wynn alone could have established all the necessary institutions, as could the wealth of the industrialists of the late nineteenth century. As far as I am aware, only one writer about visual culture prior to the Great War pointed out why Watkin Williams Wynn and the rest were not moved to create such institutions, and he was a politician, T.E. Ellis: 'I think one may say at the start—and one admits it with

[7] *Welsh Anvil*, 1950, p.39.

sorrow as well as with frankness—that not the most patriotic of us can claim for Wales the possession of a native school of art, such as is possessed in other small countries *which have obtained and enjoyed the priceless gift of self-government*'.[8]

Art patronage was manifested in the same places as power in the eighteenth and nineteenth centuries, (a conjunction not always to be assumed today). As far as Wales was concerned for most of this period, power lay in London. The early twentieth-century history of Wales demonstrates clearly—as that of Manchester, Liverpool and Birmingham before it in England—what can happen in art culture when power shifts. Industrial and shipping interests made Cardiff an economic centre of world significance before the Great War. It is not a coincidence that one of the people whose power base lay there, the Marquis of Bute, commissioned two of the most extraordinary and ambitious art works of the nineteenth century at Cardiff Castle and Castell Coch. The Church of England, under pressure from the rise of Nonconformity, also began to get its act together in Cardiff at Llandaf. As a result, Welsh artists began to emerge through Cardiff for the first time, including Milo ap Griffith, Goscombe John, Edgar Thomas and Margaret Lindsay Williams.

At the same time as Cardiff's economic significance and size increased there was a growth everywhere in public services and administration. The two combined to make Cardiff City Council a significant governmental institution with both a large budget and aspirations to play a national role in competition with other towns in Wales. Lord Aberdare, another of the rich industrialists of the area, was moved by similar national aspirations. The coming together of wealth and government in Lord Aberdare and Cardiff City Council produced the first (and still the most important) piece of public Welsh national academic art, the Pantheon of National Heroes, completed in 1916. It is the peculiarity of Wales that this national work had to be located in what is best described as a quasi-national building, the headquarters of the largest governmental institution in the country at the time, Cardiff City Hall.

The City Hall was joined by one of the only two truly national buildings of Wales, the National Museum, in 1927, but that too was the product of the same brief period before the Great War when

[8] *Young Wales*, 1899, p.145. My underlining.

significant economic and administrative power was focussed in the private and public sector in Cardiff. The role of Cardiff City Council was quite crucial to its establishment.

As Tom Ellis perceived, the relative failure of academic art in Wales was the consequence of the location of government in England. Patronage was merely an absent intermediary consequent on the same fundamental cause.[9] The position has not changed and will not change until we overcome our uncritical acceptance of the virtues of English government and accept that an indigenous culture and a particular identity are not sustainable without a parallel political expression.

b. THE NATIONAL SOUL

By the turn of the twentieth century most art intellectuals espoused the view that what they perceived as the failure of art in Wales was the consequence of a national soul not naturally suited to visual expression. In fact, they regarded the failure not so much as a specifically visual one but rather as a failure of material culture generally, which included the visual arts.

The construction of the literary and musical traditions had been a resounding success. In 1885, Cornwallis West, a leading campaigner for visual art, had remarked that the Welsh nature was 'essentially amenable to the influence of music'. In his lecture on *Art Culture in Wales* of that year he did not need to 'dwell on the two sublime branches of the arts in which Welshmen for centuries past have excelled, viz., music and poetry'. These matters were well understood and uncontroversial.

Nearly forty years later the flamboyant Clough Williams-Ellis was still expounding the same theory, at some length: 'In certain arts the Welsh of course excel—as orators and singers for example—and I am persuaded that they understand that greatest art of *living* better than the English, because they are less material. They are more fulfilled because they exercise and use their emotions and imaginations. The Englishman is more concerned about delighting

[9] The absence of an urban centre, which has also frequently been referred to, is ultimately, like the absence of patronage, the result of having no government and no governmental institutions.

his eye and his stomach, his body generally, and his material prosperity.

'Now here I think we have a clue to the poverty of the Celtic races in the visual arts generally, and architecture in particular. I can imagine the Celt arguing thus—"What can be more purely utilitarian or material than a mere building? True, our immortal souls must temporarily inhabit bodies, and our bodies, such as they are, must have shelter of some sort, but do not let us waste our precious time on such temporal and irksome necessities; let us build with our left hands, so that our right hands are still free to beat time to the hymn that we sing with our mouths"'.[10]

By the beginning of the twentieth century the national soul—variously Welsh or Celtic—had been described in detail: romantic, emotional and imaginative rather than cerebral, concerned always with the spiritual rather than the material. As an individual, the owner of this soul was apt to display the negative side of these qualities by being volatile and independent-minded. In retrospect Welsh visual artists—just as much, if not more than Welsh poets—could be shown always to have manifested these characteristics. Pennant had remarked of the Welshness of Inigo Jones that 'The turn of his countenance and the violence of his passions at least legitimate no distant descent'. Similar volatility and querrulousness was noted by a contemporary even in the arch-Classicist Richard Wilson: 'If anything occurred in conversation that displeased him, being very susceptible of hasty impressions he soon took fire, and would drop expressions of asperity which would frequently offend those who did not know him . . . This irrascible habit has been supposed to be the effect of climate, as there is no word in the Welsh language to express argument or ratiocination but contention'.

In the twentieth century Augustus John and indeed Clough Williams-Ellis were adept at this same role-play. Their pastiche Welsh bohemian greatly endeared them to the English among whom they lived.

This other-wordly national soul was a potent and fundamentally important political metaphor, constructed to make a virtue of a necessity. Ironically for a soul only able to express itself in music

[10] 'The Teaching of Art and Architecture in Wales', *Transactions of the Honourable Society of Cymmrodorion*, 1924.

and poetry, its most powerful symbolic representation—the Last Bard—was highly visual.[11] The image of the Last Bard was developed from the late seventeenth-century representation of a druid, turned more particularly Welsh by its transformation through the medium of Thomas Gray's poem of 1757. Long after the poem itself had lost its currency, the seminal images of Thomas Jones, of 1774, of Philippe de Loutherbourg at the end of the century, and of Garth Jones in 1909, with all their numerous variants from academic art to kitsch, carried the icon live into the present day.

Wales, in the person of the Last Bard, had refused to surrender her freedom to Edward I. Rather than submit to his will, the Bard had chosen to make his own death, which was, of course, not an end but the beginning of life on another and higher plane. A spiritual Wales, above this material world, led an eternal life of freedom beyond the reach of earth-bound tyranny. This is how Thomas Matthews, the leading art critic at the turn of the twentieth century, put it: 'The true character of Wales was hidden from the enemy—only to the children of her own breast was it manifest—that is, the spirit of *cynghanedd,* of rhyme and of song. These virtues do not shine in a nation which has lost its freedom, more than they are to be seen in a man who has no soul'.[12]

Matthews wrote in 1911, the year of the investiture of the Prince of Wales, the ultimate symbol that time had washed away tyranny and that England recognized the worthiness of Wales. The romantic Welsh soul, disembodied in the thirteenth century, had finally come to rest in the material body of the pragmatic English. Welsh soul and English body were reunited to form the complete and triumphant British personality. Without each other, they were incomplete.

The absolute necessity for the maintenance of this bardic metaphor of political union in the minds of Anglophile patriots presented a considerable paradox to the many enthusiasts for visual art in their ranks. The cultural implications which, while explaining our poor performance, seemed to lock the nation permanently into music and poetry and estrange it from visual art, were disagreeable. The answer to the problem lay in education. If the national soul was

[11] See Peter Lord, 'Y Bardd—Celtiaeth a Chelfyddyd', *Cof Cenedl,* 1992.
[12] *Cymru,* 1911, p.19.

not naturally disposed to art, the mind could at least be trained. Art education became the central plank in the campaigns of these individuals from Cornwallis West in the 1860s to the painter Carey Morris in the 1920s and beyond.

c. THE NATIONAL RELIGION

In 1883 the sculptor Milo ap Griffith appealed to the National Eisteddfod to 'nationalise the plastic and graphic arts, and to dispel the vulgar notion it is sometimes associated with idolatry'. Eight years later the painter Samuel Maurice Jones echoed his perception of public consciousness, remarking that 'The Puritanical spirit is so strong that she [art] is looked upon with a degree of suspicion as regards her purpose, and we suspect that we might attribute to this the fact that she is known as a bird of indeterminate hue from a foreign land that can find no sustenance on the table of the Celt'.

S.M. Jones was the son of a minister and particularly exercised by what he regarded as Nonconformst attitudes to art. He remembered one 'old saint' being 'extremely troublesome on hearing that I was beginning to study the arts. He felt strongly that the church authorities should turn their attention to the matter, and that those responsible for doctrine should look into the case. Did not the scripture say, and that in the Ten Commandments—the law of moral and eternal life and salvation—"Thou shalt not make unto thee any graven image"'.[13]

A number of artists like Jones expanded such incidents into a general theory of continuing Nonconformist iconoclasm in the search for a non-political explanation for the failure of art. It should have been necessary only to observe that academic art in Calvinist Scotland had not suffered a similar fate to academic art in Wales to see that putting the blame for the visual handicap on Nonconformity was a nonsense. It is true that Wales had experienced the destruction of church sculpture and painting in the seventeenth century, and the occasional verbal onslaughts of Puritans and puritanical Nonconformists into the nineteenth century, but this was no different to the experience of Scotland or England.

[13] Unidentified newspaper cutting in S.M.Jones' scrapbook, Gwynedd Archives, Caernarfon.

Although it took a little time for Nonconformists to become prominent amongst the nation's intelligentsia outside the confines of religion, when they did become active in the Societies and the Eisteddfod movement from the late eighteenth century they showed no reluctance to participate in the commissioning of portraits, medals, portrait sculpture and landscape painting. Indeed, as the denominations, and in particular the Calvinistic Methodists, grew into significant national institutions through the nineteenth century they generated their own institutional art. The visual culture of Nonconformity, expressed in architecture, in public sculpture, and in popular art, while not formally unique to Wales, was certainly much more fully expressed here than in England and has a national significance quite unlike anywhere else.

Ordinary chapel-goers showed no inhibitions about visual imagery. Carey Morris, in his *Art and Religion in Wales,* remembered that when he was a boy, 'it was a familiar sight to see itinerant vendors displaying most gaudy and highly-coloured reproductions of religious pictures to the simple country folk. The vendors were invariably sons of Israel and the pictures were obviously Roman Catholic in sentiment; the subjects were the Madonna and Child and the Crucifixion, very gaudily coloured and the general effect considerably heightened and made most attractive to the people by a liberal supply of gold and silver tinsel decoration. As a boy these pictures and the itinerant visitors fascinated me. Some years later it struck me a most remarkable sight—Jewish vendors selling Roman Catholic pictures to Nonconformists'.

If there was a supply-side problem it was certainly not doctrinal in origin. Nonconformists were to be found amongst artists of every kind in nineteenth-century Wales. Hugh Hughes, in the first half of the century, was a Methodist and played an important role in creating the imagery which made the preacher into an icon of the culture. The sculptors Edward Griffith and William Davies were both Methodists and responsible for those public celebrations of later establishment Methodism, the statues of Daniel Rowland and Thomas Charles. Robert Hughes, the most important naive painter of the nineteenth century in Wales, Evan Williams, an artisan portraitist turned landscape painter and art writer, and the Academy-trained portraitist William Jones, were all ministers, the first two with the Calvinistic Methodists and the third with the Wesleyans. The art enterpreneur, Hugh Humphreys of Caernarfon, publisher of quantities of landscape and national portrait prints, employer of portrait painters, copyists, and photographic studio proprietor, was a prominent Nonconformist in Caernarfon and a lay-preacher.

Hugh Humphreys' market, and that of the artisan painters who emerged in late eighteenth and early nineteenth-century Wales, was based in the new middle-class of the country, one of whose main characteristics was its Nonconformity. Neither did inconoclasm affect gentry patronage in Wales any more than in other countries. The gentry, on the whole, were not Nonconformists. In fact it was one of the few gentry families that did deviate from the Established Church that produced the most important Welsh academic painter of the later eighteenth century, Thomas Jones of Pencerrig.

IV. THE PATRIOTIC RESPONSE

Having apportioned the blame in these several ways, intellectual opinion polarized into positive and negative thinking camps in its response to the problem.

a. THE IDOLATRY OF THE WORD

The defeatist response involved making a virtue out of the apparent necessity, and abdicating collectively from a concern with visual culture. Visual ignorance came to be presented almost as a qualification for Welshness, and the greater the ignorance the greater the Welshness. Conversely, anyone showing visual tendencies was likely to come under immediate suspicion as a revisionist or fellow-traveller. This intellectually impoverished response never proceeded beyond the superficially appealing analysis—based mainly on weight of numbers—that art was an English phenomenon and that its Welsh tentacles were Anglicising in effect.

I recall the poet Euros Bowen's reaction in a meeting of the Welsh Academy to an idea designed to encourage the growth of an indigenous critique of visual culture. He sarcastically dismissed the efforts of Welsh-speaking artists—described by the archaism *'y celfyddydwyr hyn'*—as utterly peripheral, clearly convinced that his ignorance of their work and even of their names confirmed in the minds of his peers his own centrality, and the centrality of his form, in the indigenous culture. This seemed to me to be more of a demonstration of the very thing he sought to present as the problem of others and not of himself—a mind ultimately conditioned by the perceptions of the competing culture. Aggressive tone in no way made up for what was essentially defeatism. Making a virtue out of the negative consequences of colonialism in a culture simply confirms the culture in its colonized condition.[14]

The corollary of the dismissal of visual culture as a manifestation of Englishness within the national language wall, displayed by the defeatists, has been the elevation of the word to an almost religious status, and the sanctification of its exponents. Expressing pride in the indigenous literary tradition is one thing, but that tradition seems to have carried live into the twentieth century the notion of the status of the Bard in Celtic society as the unique seer of the culture, which is quite another. He, and latterly she, is uncritically afforded this status of seer even when uttering a trite two-line epigram or a limerick on *Talwrn y Beirdd.*

Nonconformist Christian attitudes also contribute to the excessively elevated status of the poet at the expense of the makers of visual images, although not, as I have pointed out, as a result of iconoclasm. Nonconformity brought to the national culture the notion of the sanctity of the Word of God in the Bible, which early on extended itself into a sort of superstitious instinct for written words of any sort. The mechanism for this was the characteristic Nonconformist association of spiritual progress with material progress. Words—the word of the Bible, and words as a medium of worldly education—were the source of both. Since education was a matter of words, it had become a great icon in Wales well before the Blue Books put it to the front of everyone's consciousness. Indeed, had it not already been such an article of faith, the suggestion that the nation was a disastrous failure educationally would have had

[14] According to Gwyn Thomas in 'Euros Bowen', *Dyrnaid o Awduron Cyfoes,* ed. D. Ben Rees, 1975, during his higher education in Llanelli he won a scholarship to Llanelli Art School, 'where he learnt something of painting'.

nowhere near as traumatic an effect. The centrality of words was promulgated paradoxically even in the benighted visual culture. I have already noted the creation of the Bard icon, but the word itself was also celebrated. The painter Hugh Hughes, in his didactic frontispiece to the new radical *Cymro* of 1830, had as the focus of all the components of contemporary Welsh culture, from cromlech to factory, a pen.

One of the inheritors of the radical and progressive Nonconformity of the *Cymro*, Samuel Roberts of Llanbrynmair, although pleased as editor of the *Cronicl* to include a review of the Manchester Art Exhibition of 1867, nevertheless felt obliged to add a cautionary foreword concerning writing and painting. Although 'the two arts are similar to each other—writing is the more useful', he reminded his readers. 'Usefulness' as a package—spiritual and temporal—had become a resonant war-cry, a central theme in nineteenth-century Nonconformist theology.

Painting was certainly not considered useful. Rather than a revival of seventeenth-century iconoclasm, Nonconformity contributed to the culture a new idolatry of the word, worshipped as the means of spiritual salvation and material prosperity. Indeed, in the mouth of the Bard and the Preacher, two deeply interwoven icons of the culture, the word—almost any word—was sanctified.

b. A SURROGATE TRADITION

i. A tradition of contribution

Intellectuals of a different turn of mind, disposed for a variety of reasons not to devalue visual culture, responded rather differently. John Gibson's international reputation—he was declared unequivocally to be 'the world's most eminent sculptor' on his death in 1866 by the *Art Journal*—was to them a reminder in the nineteenth century of what Wilson had suggested in the eighteenth, that the notion of a congenital Welsh visual handicap was an unjustified slight. The lesser presence of Penry Williams at Gibson's side confirmed that indeed the national soul was disposed to love beauty. The appeal of these two in Wales itself was increased by their having risen so high from humble origins, emphasising the virtue of self-improvement through education, the route to national as well as personal salvation. Reviews of this period often emphasise this point. The *Carnarvon and Denbigh Herald* ventured a highly suggestive parallel which all but sanctified Joseph Edwards in 1855, saying that 'The sculptor, with the well-known Mr Evan Thomas, is a specimen of a self-educated artizan who has ascended from the carpenter's bench to the chisel, and to the brush and palette of the artist'. In 1860, in response to a tirade delivered by John Francis of Manchester, an enthusiastic Eisteddfod reformer and promoter of visual culture, Sir Watkin Williams Wynn noted 'in a playful mood' that 'when a country like this one can be the birth-place of a Gibson and a Wilson, I may say we are not so very much disgraced'.

This reaction against the congenital incapacity theory was given an extra dimension from the 1880s on when national consciousness was rising to its shaky political peak, by the campaigning of the painter and writer T.H. Thomas for the recognition of 'the only indigenous art of Wales', that is, Celtic Christian art. As we have seen, this work was well-known to the antiquarians, and Pennant had even ventured the word 'beautiful' to describe one example of it, a daring (but isolated) remark in an age when the word had very particular meanings and associations in art culture.[15] However, it required a change of aesthetics to bring it generally out of archaeology and into the realm of art. The new utilitarian age saw art as informing industrial and domestic design. Christian Celtic art was a 'rational' art, that is, it was geometric and perceived as ornamental in purpose and Owen Jones, the son of Owain Myfyr, had included examples of it—including Welsh examples—in his seminal *Grammar of Ornament* in 1856. However, it was the publication of *The Book of Kells* in facsimile in the 1880s which stimulated the stylistic Celtic revival which lasted into the 1920s.

The climate was right for a first attempt at the construction of a tradition which would undermine the myth of the visual handicap. Unfortunately, the prestige of contemporary English art was also at a high point at the turn of the century—indeed, it was largely from that prestige that London-orientated Welsh intellectuals and artists drew their confidence. This suggested that the most appealing and prestigious tradition for Wales would be a *tradition of contribution* to the great English art culture. As Wales had given her romantic

[15] *Tours in Wales*, 1883 edition, p.18. Pennant is talking about the 'Maen Achwyfan'.

poetic soul to the new compound Britain, as sister to sister, so her visual artists had contributed to the tradition of English art. This was plainly the case, as the position of Wilson in that tradition demonstrated. All that was needed, as with the nation's contribution as a whole, was recognition of the fact that Wilson was a Welshman, and a substantial blow for national pride and self-esteem would have been struck.

Art—unlike politics, where the slippery semantics of 'Britain' were often skillfully employed—was in this period almost invariably and unequivocally English, never British. Only exceptionally did even Welsh patriots exercise any care in making distinctions, and then, as in the case of Isaac Williams, the first Keeper of Art at the National Museum, writing in the 1920s, it did not alter the essential contributory critique: 'If we consider the development of art in England from a purely historical standpoint—which is by far the most interesting and attractive method by which students and the general public can approach it—we shall find that Welshmen played a very prominent and distinguished part in the history of architecture, painting and the minor arts. It is full time that these hitherto obscure men, their work, and above all, their nationality, should be more widely known not only throughout Wales, but wherever the influence of Welshmen may be felt'.

What was required was to build up around the core of Wilson and Gibson, and in architecture Inigo Jones, a cast of supporting players, all legitimised by having had careers in the English academic art world. The net was thrown as widely as possible within this narrow confine.

A Welsh artist was defined by family ancestry, by place of birth, or by place of work if that was predominantly Wales. This was by no means an unreasonable set of parameters for the time—it was, indeed, precisely the parameters which English art historians (and musicologists) had used to include continental painters such as Holbein and Van Dyke (and musicians such as Handel and Mendelssohn) in the great construct of English cultural tradition which retains its currency in the English consciousness to this day.

This collection of artists was put together in tangible form first by the Reverend D. Mardy Rees in 1909 in his book *Welsh Painters, Engravers, and Sculptors,* a landmark in Welsh visual culture. Mardy

Rees was in fact primarily a compiler—the material for the book had been collected by several artists and art enthusiasts including T. C. Evans (Cadrawd) and T. H. Thomas. However, the identification of a number of artists, sharing only their relative success in the English art world, hardly constituted a credible Welsh tradition on its own, especially as their identification as Welsh was so variable. This was a list rather than a story.

ii. The Celtic soul in the landscape

The artists were bound together into a tradition by the writers of the pre-war period by the perception in their works of that characteristic national soul which similarly manifested itself ambiguously as both an integral part and as a distinct entity in the wider context of British nationhood. Making this perception credible required considerable aesthetic gymnastics as the contributions of the two most notable exemplers of the tradition were at variance with the stereotype, being distinctly unromantic and Last Bard-like. John Gibson's contribution to the freedom struggle of the Italians in Rome in 1848 had not been substantial: 'I ran away', he noted in a letter to Mrs Sandbach, Hafod-un-nos.

Similarly, the other great Welsh classicist, Richard Wilson, had to be transformed in the minds of most writers in the pursuit of a coherent aesthetic, expressive of the romantic national soul. Writing as recently as 1938, Edmund D. Jones described him as 'the most Welsh in his spirit and style of them all'.[16] This bizarre notion of Wilson's work as expressive of turbulence and the love of freedom was, surprisingly, not entirely confined to patriotic Welsh prejudice. Such was his reputation at the beginning of the nineteenth century that Fuseli was also moved to claim him as a progenitor of his particular romantic aesthetics: 'Though in effects of dewy freshness, and silent evening light, few have equalled and fewer excelled him, his grandeur is oftener allied to terror, bustle, and convulsion, than to calmness and tranquility'.

In fact, the nature of Richard Wilson's painting could safely be ignored by this time as the myth of the man himself as an archetypal Celt had largely superceded it. Fortunately, as I have pointed out, he

[16] *Camre Celfyddyd*, Gwasg Aberystwyth, 1938.

had been observed by his contemporaries to be of excitable Welsh temperament, and his career became a metaphor for the condition of the nation. According to the great authority of Ruskin, he had founded the English School of landscape painting, a cornerstone of English art culture, indeed of English self-perception, yet he—like the nation itself in 1847—had been rejected in his own lifetime by those to whom he had given everything, and so declined into obscurity and penury. He had died in the bosom of his own native land, which alone had given him succour at the end. The myth of Richard Wilson grew to such proportions that in 1889 Isaac Foulkes could describe him as 'our only Welsh painter'.[17]

The expatriate English painters of Welsh landscape, achieving a new peak of fashion in the wake of the mid-century popularity of David Cox, presented a different problem of assimilation. In so far as Welsh visual culture existed to the outside world at all it was Welsh landscape painting—Wales seen, not Wales seeing. This was unsatisfactory, but an inescapable fact which by the end of the nineteenth century was heavily reinforced by the bent of the popular poets, and so it became necessary to nationalise the product in some way. Wales, like it or not, would have to see through the eyes of this landscape, so closely bound by then to the poetic soul of the nation, in the work of the artists of the '*Arlunfa Gymreig*', the Welsh studio.

It was from a group of these expatriates working in Cox's shadow in Dyffryn Conwy that the original idea for a Cambrian Academy had emanated. T. H. Thomas, sensing the danger, involved himself in an effort to nationalise the movement, being 'deeply anxious that, in the building up of an institution destined to do a most valuable work in Wales, national art and national artists should hold their due place both numerically and by merit'.[18] He found it hard going—some prominent Welsh artists of the time preferred to keep away, their London associations not to be diluted by 'regional' affiliations. Thomas Matthews, in support of T. H. Thomas, nationalised not only the movement but the painters themselves. Writing of the primogenitor, David Cox, he noted that 'although he was born near Worcester on the Severn, the Goddess of the river

[17] *Y Traethodydd*, 1889.

[18] 'The Royal Cambrian Academy of Art', *Y Cymrodor*, VIII, 1884.

had, as it were, given him an instinct to look to the mountains of his country for strength. Like many others he came to her breast and received bountiful gifts'. Among Matthews's contemporaries the painter B. W. Leader reigned supreme; only Cox surpassed him by showing more obviously his 'Celtic origins'. Matthews re-baptised David Cox as Dafydd Coch and B.W. Leader as B.W. Elidyr.[19]

iii. Plus ça change

The spirit of the Goddess, transmitted by blood rather than water, manifested herself in the work of the third constituent of the new tradition, the artists of Welsh ancestry, and none more so than Burne-Jones. To Edmund D. Jones 'The characteristics of the Celt are easy to perceive in his pictures. The spiritual and poetic elements are obvious, and the lively imagination that is the inheritance of our nation'. In Mardy Rees's book, only Wilson and Gibson were eulogised on the level of Burne-Jones. He quotes another of his Celts, Watts, as the final authority: '"I was one day sitting with Watts in his studio", remembered C. E. Hallé, "and he said to me: 'Whereabouts in art do you place Burne-Jones?'" "Amongst the first twelve or fifteen", I replied. 'I place him first of all', said Watts"'.

In *Art in Wales* Eric Rowan mocked Mardy Rees in the patronising tones of one who considered himself to have transcended 'an insular, regional viewpoint' through a broad, international vision of art. Mardy Rees's critique had 'a directness and authority that Duchamp would have envied', he snidely remarked. In fact, Rowan's critique for *Art in Wales* was precisely the same as that used by Mardy Rees. His narrow frame was academic art—'folk art has been excluded'[20]—and the main condition for inclusion was contribution to the English art tradition, thinly disguised as 'the mainstream of modern art'. Only the definition of Welsh artist was changed, though that, in practice, precious little. The racist connotations which to pinkish intellectuals of the 1960s adhered to definition by blood-line were not acceptable. Unfortunately, the

[19] *Cymru*, 1911, p.209.

[20] This comment was made in Vol.I of *Art in Wales*, p.11, of which Rowan was editor. The writer was John Ingamells, reflecting a decision originally made in connection with the exhibition 'Art in Wales', 1964, on which the first volume of the book was based.

poverty of Rowan's own critique led to a distinct shortage of acceptable art to show in his book, and so the likes of Frank Brangwyn, blood or not, were granted admission to make up the numbers. This was justified on the grounds of convention—the convention which had been created by the parochial and quasi-racist Mardy Rees, of course, and which had been confirmed by the new National Museum's seminal exhibition of 1913, 'Modern Artists of Welsh Birth or Extraction'.

c. NATIONAL ART INSTITUTIONS

i. Conflicting aspirations

Despite the influential support of T. H. Thomas, the Royal Cambrian Academy, like the Eisteddfod before it, failed as a national art institution. A quarter of a century later T. H. Thomas and his patriotic generation, and in particular Goscombe John, the most highly regarded Welsh artist of the period, achieved the foundation of a third national art institution, the Art Department of the new National Museum.

National museums are one of the most important expressions of nineteenth-century nationalism, and Wales was slow, in European terms, to acquire this central symbol of identity. The charter was granted in 1907 but the Museum did not open its doors to the public in its own building until 1927.

The normally straightforward symbolism of a national museum, intended for both internal and external consumption, is uniquely confused in the cases of Wales and Scotland by their British status. The council of the National Museum of Wales was well aware of this and, at the outset and in theory, clear as to what to do about it: 'It is intended that the new Museum shall be primarily and essentially National in character. Its special and characteristic function must, according to the views of its Council, be to teach the stranger about Wales and to teach the Welsh people about their own country. Above all things, it must not attempt to be a copy of the British Museum on a small scale which happens to be situated in Wales . . . Nothing should be admitted . . . which does not illustrate or elucidate Wales in some aspect or other'. These strong and clear words were taken from the programme of the opening ceremony of the building–yet that opening was, of course, carried out by the British monarch, George V.

The aspirations of the Museum in 1927 were still therefore those of the art patriots of the 1880s generation. Similarly, the abject failure of its Art Department to fulfill those aspirations would be rooted in the ambiguity of their patriotism expressed in visual art in their vision of a tradition of contribution by Welsh artists to the English art culture. Those Anglocentric politics and culture critique have not changed and have gradually neutralised any residual national aspiration. The situation inside the Museum has reflected closely the situation in art history on the outside. The stagnation of critique and gradual abandonment of the national commitment from Mardy Rees, through Bell to Rowan on the outside, has been expressed inside in the succession of Keepers from Isaac Williams, through Rollo Charles and Peter Cannon-Brookes, to Timothy Stevens.

A catalogue note of the Art Department's policy, published the year before the opening, clearly stated the ultimately self-defeating contributive critique which the Museum would expound, and also the role of material drawn from other cultures: 'The primary object of the Art Department is to illustrate the artistic achievements of the Welsh people; to make known their contributions to the British Schools of painting, engraving and sculpture; and to bring together a collection of works representative of the principal English and continental schools of fine and applied art'.

National art museums were always established with two main aims in mind. On the one hand they were to assert the particularity of the nation they symbolised, and on the other they were to assert the high quality of its culture. Unfortunately, quality, in the minds of the kind of people who were in a position to create such institutions, was identified with high art culture, so that for some countries, whose cultures were marginal to the evolution of high art, the aims were contradictory. The need to justify their claim to be considered equally civilised within the family of western nations usually prevailed in the ensuing competition, so that they often ended up seeking to stress not the particularity of the indigenous culture but its homogeneity. This they achieved by amassing collections of European high art, demonstrative of national good taste, and by reconstructing their indigenous cultures as variants, or sub-cultures, of that mainstream.

In Wales the parameters of quality in visual culture were given by the particular Anglocentric version of European high art history. The assertion of the quality of the Welsh culture required therefore a collection of European high art, in particular English art, demonstrating national good taste, and a collection of indigenous work which mimicked its aesthetics and demonstrated the ability of its artists as contributors to that tradition. As we have seen, it was Art Department policy from the start to include non-Welsh, high art material. It was described in the general policy statement of the Museum as 'comparative', and its function was to 'elucidate' the history of Wales, but this was never its real purpose and it has never been used in this legitimate way. Its display was not intended to elucidate the indigenous culture but to evaluate the national taste for the benefit of outsiders, and in so doing act as an arbiter of good taste for insiders. The National Museum of Wales constructed Richard Wilson and John Gibson into the great Welsh exemplars of good taste exactly as the Anglophile progressives of the National Eisteddfod sought to do in the 1860s: 'Wales has contributed works of art such as those of Wilson and Gibson', remarked Chancellor Williams at Aberystwyth in 1865, 'that may well be held up to stimulate the artistic talent that may yet lie dormant in our secluded valleys, and to correct the taste of our aspirants'. It has more often than not had the opposite effect.

The demonstration of good taste on behalf of nations by the Directors of their Museums has rapidly decayed into a competition between institutions with their own collective egos as the main motive power. The relevance of their activities to the indigenous culture has become a very minor consideration. However patriotic and altruistic the motives of their founders, institutions have become primarily interested in their own prestige amongst their international peers. In this context the 'National Collection' soon becomes the museum's collection and the staff, when referring—as they often do—to 'our Van Gogh' or 'our Poussin', are excluding rather than including the rest of us. A good demonstration of this attitude was the relish with which the Keeper of Art of the National Musuem of Wales greeted the Davies Bequest in 1951: 'By this princely benefaction the character of the Department of Art has been transformed', he rejoiced, 'so that it now takes a high place among the major art-collections of Great Britain'.[21]

ii. The Davies Collection

In the early part of his career as Keeper of Art, Isaac Williams reminded the nation that Wales had previously 'been regarded as a mere episode in the general history of England'. Notwithstanding his contributory critique, he consistently emphasised the indigenous product, as defined by Mardy Rees. The acquisition of considerable numbers of works by Wilson in his period and his exhibition programme outside the Museum clearly demonstrated his patriotic intent. He used the National Eisteddfod as a medium for placing exhibitions, sometimes very large exhibitions, in schools and halls throughout Wales. These tended to combine works by Wilson and Penry Williams with works by living artists such as Christopher Williams and Augustus John. However, loans from the 1930s on of works from the collections of the Davies sisters of Gregynog, culminating in the bequests of 1951 and 1963, undermined this foundation on which, in time, a more appropriate critique for the understanding of indigenous visual culture might have been built.

The collections of the Davies sisters contained substantial numbers of late nineteenth-century paintings by the artists who have come to be absorbed into the mainstream history of European high art, including Monet, Renoir, Cézanne and Van Gogh. In 1962, by which time many of the works which formed the second bequest were already in the Museum as loans, there were 196 oil paintings on show, of which 90 came from that one source.

The bequests not only dominated hanging policy but also purchasing policy. In the 1960s and 1970s the purchase of indigenous work dwindled to almost nothing. In 1970 the bronze 'Penelope' by Bourdelle was bought specifically 'to supplement the Davies collection . . . It was thought to be an appropriate addition to their sculptures by Degas and Rodin'.

[21] This and following quotations concerning the official policy of the National Museum and the Welsh Folk Museum are taken from the *Annual Report* for the relevant year, unless otherwise stated.

The Davies bequests caused the covert redefinition of the policy of the Department in direct contravention of the stated policy of the 1920s by elevating the collection of English and continental high art to the central place. As a consequence, the internal requirements of the Davies collection—that is, its strengths and weaknesses in terms of its ability to elucidate conventional European high art history—dominated purchasing policy, rather than the needs of elucidating the indigenous culture of Wales, which were and are very different. This first occurred on a large scale with the purchase of the 'Entrance to the Grand Canal' by Canaletto, and culminated in the purchase for £7.2 million, jointly with the English National Gallery, of a Poussin in 1989. These investments are to be contrasted with the failure to acquire the two Wynnstay Wilsons, which went to the United States in 1971.

The Davies collection suddenly elevated the National Museum's Art Department to a status in the museum world that the quality of its academic staff, and their hanging, exhibition and research policies, arguably did not justify. In fact, by the time of Peter Cannon-Brookes as Keeper (1978-1986), the purchase demands of this international status had reduced the rest of the funding to an approximate level equal to that of the local district council museum service, or perhaps less. Partly as a consequence, since the second world war, the national institution has done no research, sponsored no research, and published virtually nothing relating to the study of the visual culture in Wales, other than brief catalogue introductions. The only exception is Steegman's portrait survey which remains, with all its deficiencies, the Museum's one and only written contribution to the study of this important subject.

On several occasions during the period of office of Peter Cannon-Brookes the media focused its attention on the institution, and in the eyes of many observers the National Museum became a byeword for incompetence and a laughing-stock. The international life-style of the Keeper and his purchase of tapestry cartoons doubtfully attributed to Rubens, contributed to his departure. Furthermore, it has been claimed that the controversies associated with Cannon-Brookes contributed to the early retirement of the Museum's Director in 1985 and his replacement by the former secretary, a choice which surprised some members of staff given the quality of some of the other candidates. Things did not improve and the situation finally moved the Secretary of State at that time, Nicholas Edwards, to act. The result was the Hudson Davies report, the published part of which dealt with 'Housing the Visual Arts in Wales'.

The report was a crucial failure. The desire of Nicholas Edwards to make a grand gesture of high art patronage ensured that the quality of the Museum in terms of British institutions—the only institutions with which comparisons were made—dominated the conclusions. The report made fundamental assumptions which were quite inappropriate to the development of the indigenous culture whose continued existence gives the Museum its only *raison d'être* as a national institution. It assumes throughout that the nation in question is Britain, that Cardiff is a regional centre, and that the requirements of Welsh people are the same as the requirements of English people. Nowhere is the Welsh national context mentioned, the exposition of the story of this nation, or the role of the institution in developing a distinct national life.

The blueprint was for what the founders of the Museum had specifically warned against: 'a copy of the British Museum on a small scale which happens to be situated in Wales'. In order to 'greatly enrich' what the report repeatedly pointed out was a third-rate collection, substantial loans from the Tate Gallery were to be made. What was proposed, and what is coming to pass at a cost of £24 million, is a conservative, mainstream British institution, conceptually indistinguishable (apart from a token regional bias in the works displayed) from any national art museum in London. The exposition of the particular qualities of the indigenous culture has been totally eliminated from its aims. The opportunity to invest in the indigenous culture and to put it on the world map by adventurous and creative interpretation through the application of an appropriate critique of visual culture for a small nation has been thrown away.

iii. Sain Ffagan

It became apparent early in the history of the new Museum building that the aspiration of the Museum to be 'national in character' was not being met. Even with Isaac Williams's enthusiasm for Welsh artists, the contributory critique of the Department reinforced the foreignness of visual art. The other Department chiefly concerned with material culture, Archaeology, dealing substantially with pre-Welsh material, seemed equally remote. The largest part of the material culture of Wales was without a spiritual home.

In 1930 the Director, Cyril Fox, visited open-air museums in Scandinavia, at the time the latest thing in the museum world. On his return he reported that 'the museum service in Wales is incomplete without illustration of the Welsh culture-complex such as can only be afforded by an open-air field museum'. The aspiration to build such a museum was incorporated into policy.

The critique which had generated the open-air museums was one which recognized the marginality of Scandinavian nations to imperial political and economic power and to high art culture. In Wales, as we have seen, progressive patriots had sought to drag the country into this prestigious context on Mother England's coat-tails. Scandinavian nationalist intellectuals responded differently, seeking to elevate as a national mainstream the particularity of the main body of the indigenous material culture even though it lay outside what was valued by high art critique. In the process they established an alternative value-system and aesthetics. These indigenous cultures were defined by the term 'folk'. Therefore the National Museum was, in 1931, not so much adopting the idea of an open-air museum as adopting a folk-culture critique for the particular evaluation of the indigenous culture: 'It was urged that the importance of the material illustrating the life and work of the people of Wales, now possessed by the museum, should be emphasised by a descriptive name such as 'The Welsh Folk Collection'. Within five years this collection was separated as a new Department of Folk Culture and Industries.

The Department was to 'concern itself with the trades and crafts, the ways of living and working, the domestic and industrial environment, the clothes and customs, of our forebears of all social grades', and to 'provide the people of Wales with a source hitherto untapped of national self-knowledge'. This definition of one department's work was, with the exception of the exclusion of 'comparative material', all-encompassing and—specifically mentioning industry and 'all social grades'—little different from the stated aims of the Museum as a whole down to 1927. The national role of the National Museum was effectively being devolved onto one Department, leaving the other Departments, and particularly Art (as the one most directly concerned with material culture), with undefined policy objectives.

As we have seen, this suited the increasingly Anglicised procession of Keepers of Art after the war very well. As the Folk Culture and Industries Department grew in size and its national identification grew in strength on moving to Sain Ffagan, they were able to pursue their own inclinations without internal criticism in the direction reinforced by the Davies bequests, towards the creation of a gallery of international high art. The displays were weeded of all Welsh material save portraits of Welsh sitters by notable English artists such as Reynolds and Romney, and the high status products of Wilson and John, treated as contributory to the English tradition. Even the Celtic crosses, the fruits of T. H. Thomas's retrieval work, formerly displayed with the nineteenth-centry Welsh sculpture in the entrance hall, were removed to a side gallery with archaeology and thus isolated from the rest of the visual culture—a move of great symbolic significance.

In the meantime Sain Ffagan resolved the ambiguity within the original definition of its role as being at the same time both folk-based and as including industry and 'all social grades', in favour of a narrower definition of folk culture, strongly emphasising rural communities and craft, and the related social classes. To what extent this reflects an evolution in the philosophy of the intellectual force behind the Folk Museum, Iorwerth Peate, is unclear. Certainly in the 1930s Peate's approach was holistic. 'Folk culture as a museum subject is a study of the mental, spiritual, and material struggle of the whole community; none is excluded', he wrote. 'To equate "folk life" with "lower class" is a fundamental misconception'.[22]

Despite the presence of the castle, with its examples of aristocratic patronage, within the Folk Museum, there is little interpretation of the interaction between the material culture of the

[22] 'The Place of Folk Culture in the Museum', *The Museums Journal*, June 1941, vol. 41.

aristocracy and the objects classified by association in the other buildings and in the museum displays, as Folk. There is a complete absence of interpretation of interactions between the material culture of urban and often expatriate Welsh art intellectuals, and the bulk of the collection.

Iorwerth Peate considered academic art as quite peripheral to his concept of the essential Welsh culture. He rejected, with some disdain, Saunders Lewis's attempts to construct Wales into the classical European mainstream.[23] Whilst it would be an exaggeration to suggest that Peate—a great internationalist as well as a patriot—saw no value in the European high art tradition, there was, in his character, an ever-present tension between the rational and the emotional which allowed a vague but deeply felt prejudice against academic art to manifest itself on occasions. He perceived academic art as 'highbrow' and inconsistent with his image of a classless and self-sustaining Welsh folk. He seemed to feel that artists were foreign by class and nationality. He often expressed his contempt for the theorising which he associated with sophisticated art. The truth is that he himself was a theorist and his contribution to the aesthetics of material culture was by far the greatest of any Welsh person of his generation.

It might seem odd to suggest that the richness of the visual material at Sain Ffagan, well shown and in a Welsh context supported by many staff with a commitment to the indigenous culture, has done nothing to undermine the notion of a national visual handicap, but this is, regrettably, the case. At Sain Ffagan this material is not projected as being part of a visual culture, which remains damned by association with that English phenomenon of visual art. Art is rejected, and in its place rural craft is sanctified as a truly Welsh phenomenon. Visual material is indiscriminately presented as if it were the product of convention. Images as an active element in changing thought—as new ideas and aspirations—are present largely by default at Sain Ffagan, as indeed are ideas and aspirations themselves. Sain Ffagan presents to the ordinary visitor, not disposed to read every caption, a society without intellectual life, opinions and politics,

[23] 'Traddodiad Ewrop', *Y Llenor*, 1936.

possessing only customs. For instance, Pen-rhiw chapel was restored to the condition it had when first converted to religious use from a barn. This was a manifestation of a radical change in Welsh society, based on ideas whose newness led to repression and accusations of sedition, and which was central to the invention of a new Wales rather than to the continuation of an old one. Yet in the context of the Folk Museum, Pen-rhiw chapel suggests a tradition which seems to ordinary visitors to have been already centuries old, rather than a social revolution.

Sain Ffagan locks Wales into a perpetual rural past and as the general western fashion for 'heritage' grows in strength, the ghettoisation of Wales as a narrowly defined folk culture becomes an increasingly potent force acting against the living culture. There seem to be few implications for now in what is presented and certainly no organic development into now. Wales has come to an end at some indeterminate point in the nineteenth century, a passive nation exisiting in a time warp. It is a concluded story.[24] The unself-conscious flow that can link the material culture of the past and the present in a confident and politically independent culture is inhibited. The development of design in Scandanavia in the 1950s, thoroughly new but informed by the tradition constructed out of the folk critique of the open-air museums there, has had no parallel here. Reference back in contemporary Welsh visual culture, in this context of a ghettoised past, almost always seems to be an artificial historicism.

As well as by Pen-rhiw chapel, Nonconformity is represented by prints on the walls of several buildings at Sain Ffagan, but these objects too are traditionalised by the folk context. They are not, in fact, folk objects at all, but pieces of popular art, produced outside the conventions of the rural culture and related to new and fashionable ideas common to a social structure of far wider extent than the rural folk confines of Sain Ffagan. The interaction of ideas within the social groups of the culture is not interpreted at Sain Ffagan, any more that it is at Cathays Park. We have a polarization between two incomplete critiques. In the presentation of visual culture there is no suggestion of the

[24] The re-erection of the terrace of houses from Merthyr and other recent developments suggest that this attitude may be changing.

relationship of the images presented in a rural folk context to their sources in urban popular art and in high art. By ignoring this interaction the critique at Sain Ffagan reinforces the division of visual culture into a foreign high art culture and a separate indigenous craft culture, with all its damaging consequences. In many ways, Peate reproduced a sophisticated version of the mentality of the antiquarians of the eighteenth and early nineteenth centuries. The Welsh part of Welsh culture is a kind of living archaeology, represented at Sain Ffagan by contemporary exponents of craft skills, while the modern world in Wales is English, represented by the aesthetics of the Art Department at Cathays Park. Not only is displayed material in the two museums misrepresented, but much of the appropriate material for the building of a tradition of indigenous visual culture is never seen at all, lost somewhere between the inadequate critiques of the two.

Sain Ffagan has succeeded in becoming identified as the national part of the National Museum. Its outstanding success now presents a serious difficulty for the future of the culture it was established to sustain.[25]

V. A NEW PATRIOTIC RESPONSE

a. HIGH ART AND COLONIALISM

The high art critique of which I have written so much puts the history of visual culture on a single-track tramline. The tram periodically slows down, picks up a new passenger, and speeds on in the same direction, towards the evolution of style. The tram has been rolling since the Renaissance when Vasari first encapsulated its artist-centred approach by organizing previous art into a one-way ticket from Cimabue to Michaelangelo. The tram, running on ever-extending tracks, eventually assumed a life

[25] I have not commented here on the policies of the two other national institutions with a brief which includes visual culture. I have excluded the National Library because I am mainly concerned with the perceptions of a wide public and—unfortunately—the Library remains a mainly specialist research centre in this field with a low public profile of exhibitions. I have discussed the policies of the Arts Council at length in *Cultural Policy*, 1986.

of its own, an individual following his or her own internal logic. 'Style takes on the aspect of a living being working out its destiny', as Malraux put it. However, the tramline never ran into the Welsh suburbs.

It is not a coincidence that high art critique was formed in those European cultures which developed into the imperial powers of the modern world. It was an important, and underestimated, part of the philosophical structure that legitimised and so facilitated colonialism. Internally, high art critique played a similar role in legitimising class and gender structures. Externally and internally high art critique is concerned with only a tiny part of visual culture. Its influence has been so huge because it has asserted that that part of visual culture uniquely expresses the 'highest' human values and aspirations. Those nations, those classes, and that gender with which it has been associated are by extension, therefore, superior. The culture, class, and gender-specific nature of these values of beauty and truth, have been successfully disguised by the quite contrary assertion that they are universal and stand above nationality, class, and gender.

High art critique remains dominant in the West. Other critiques, coming from folklorists or from Marxists, have been acknowledged but—despite occasional manifestations in exhibitions—effectively marginalized as contributory to this mainstream. They remain alternatives for minorities of a quirky disposition. The high art which has been selected out and ordered into a mainstream tradition has become synonymous with culture. That is to say, 'culture' means 'art'; the rest of life is something else.

In Wales, the application of an unmodified high art critique to Welsh visual culture remains a significant instrument of colonialism. Unchallenged here, it continues to devalue the indigenous work and therefore undermines the self-confidence of the nation. The United States and third-world countries have rejected this low valuation of indigenous culture and asserted their identity and independence by reassesing the philosophical basis of value—that is, by changing their culture critique. While we continue to accept the low valuation of an inappropriate critique to even one aspect of our culture, aspirations to self-determination will be fundamentally inhibited and the destruction of that which we do value accelerated.

b. THE AMERICAN EXAMPLE

The role of art in maintaining a colonialist mentality became well understood in the United States in the 1920s and 30s. A movement to assert a particular American identity challenged the unique encapsulation of the highest quality of human experience in the European high art which had so fascinated American writers and visual artists at the turn of the century. American critique began to change, rejecting the imitation of these aesthetics by American artists. By 1941 Jean Lipman could write that 'Most critics have consistently based their estimates on academic English or Continental standards, naming those American painters the greatest who were the least American and most imitative in their approach. The bold, abstract American style has been criticised as lacking in finesse of characterisation and in subtlety of coloring and design. It is a strange blindness that has caused these critics to look for skilled academic refinement in the art of a sturdy pioneering people who had colonised a wilderness through fresh vigorous enterprise and robust vitality—qualities with which the native art was necessarily endowed. But, as Willard Huntingdon Wright commented in his *Misinforming a Nation,* "in our slavish imitation of England—the only country in Europe of which we have any intimate knowledge—we have de-Americanised ourselves to such an extent that there has grown up in us a typical British contempt for our own native achievements"'.[26]

As we see, by this time American intellectuals had gone a long way towards constructing a different and compelling foundation myth for the American people which rejected the Anglocentric model. The consequence was a new aesthetics which identified an indigenous style and a spiritual foundation to account for it. The process had begun with a reaction against industrialism not dissimilar to the English Art and Craft reaction with its parallel in the folk-song movement. However, the 'sanitised Anglo-

[26] 'American Primitive Portraiture: a Revaluation', *Antiques,* 1941.

American past'[27] thus created did not withstand the stress of the Depression. Folk culture could not be contructed in the same way in the United States. It could not be seen as so essentially rural as its English model, and came instead to be focussed on the idealisation of small-town life. It also involved the notion of Pluralism—it was in the United States that the term was invented—which was a concept quite opposed to the ethnic unity of the English folk. Neither was it isolated by great age—an essential difference—being a living and developing phenomenon which could be observed and recorded in a much more complete way in the contemporary American world than in England where it was already a relic.[28]

It became apparent that artefacts consistent with the new critique of a pluralist folk culture as the mainstream American tradition extended beyond rural craft objects and included forms derived from high art culture, including especially portraiture. By association, this painting became known in the United States as Folk Painting. Once a few examples were recognised and revalued by Lipman and others, and taken up by gallery owners, connoisseurs and artists, a large body of previously unknown work began gradually to be revealed.

Although many of the ideas which moved American consciousness at this time were present in the European cultures with developed high art traditions—anti-industrialism, anti-capitalism, democratization—the high art critique was never deposed here as the mainstream. Its perception as indigenous in these countries gave it a patriotic appeal which protected it. As we have seen, in Wales—perceiving itself as a contributor to such an indigenous high art tradition—folk critique emerged not as a mainstream as in America or Scandinavia but as a marginalizing phenomenon, parcelled up as a concluded past, a sort of maiden aunt rather than a mother of us all, and devoid even in its

[27] *Folk Roots, New Roots,* ed. Jane S.Becker and Barbera Franco, 1990.

[28] This change in perception of American identity was not without its ambiguities. The heroic myth of the American Indian was created at the same time and enthusiastically appropriated as a part of the white foundation myth, even as the raw material was being persecuted out of existence. Also, at the same time as they were investing in the particularity of their identity, Americans manifested a desire for admission into the family of civilized nations by acquiring collections of European high art.

historical existence of a particular visual dimension. No indigenous portrait painting was revealed here. As late as 1978 *Art in Wales* pronounced authoritatively that 'Of the specific patronage of local talent there is little to record.'

In the United States folk painting was incorporated into fine art. It developed its own appropriate value system which revealed a hierarchy of masters such as Hicks, Phillips and North. It found its way into the consciousness of avant-garde artists and designers and became a component in the most potent visual culture in the world in the second half of the twentieth century.

I cite the experience of the United States not as a precise model for the construction of a tradition of Welsh visual culture—that would be to repeat past errors of imitation—but as a lesson in how changes of critique reveal work not previously recognized and therefore impotent in the culture. Furthermore, it shows us how the construction of a tradition from the revealed material (and the consequent re-evaluation of the previously recognized material) can stimulate the contemporary visual culture and contribute to the assertiveness and self-confidence of the nation as a whole.

c. RECOGNITION

I have noted how the parameters employed by the National Museum into the 1930s, by its own admission, excluded the bulk of 'the Welsh culture complex'. I have also noted that the version of folk critique which replaced it has been equally selective. In particular that critique has failed to place a whole range of visual images in a context which can enlighten us as to their genesis and meaning. It is inadequate as a mainstream national critique of material culture because it has failed to undermine that most negative assumption of a congenital visual inadequacy in the Welsh people.

The American experience demonstrates that the questioning of a prevalent critique must be accompanied not only by a re-examination of recognized material and ideological evidence but by a change in the parameters for the selection of that evidence. In 1986 I made a general survey of visual images in Welsh culture and related ideology which revealed immediately a number of works which by social context and, indeed, by style, were reminiscent of the recovered visual culture of the United States. For instance, there were a number of portraits of the dramatist Twm o'r Nant which, in so far as they were known at all, were familiar only to enthusiasts such as those who read the magazine *Y Casglwr*. Their status was that of Welsh curio. The marginal position of these paintings seemed to me to be inconsistent with the significance they must have had in their contemporary culture to have warranted the expense and trouble of getting them made. Indeed, no less than four paintings of Twm o'r Nant were reportedly made on a single occasion in 1810. This was not suggestive of a marginal visual culture nor consistent with the received wisdom about the scarcity of practitioners in the period. Yet neither high art nor folk art critique had a way of revealing the meaning of these paintings.

It seemed to me that the restoration of meaning to these images was dependent on their integration into a view of Welsh material culture and related ideology which recognised the interaction of high art culture (the portrait painting tradition, in this case) and a much more widely based popular consciousness, recognized in folk critique, to which the literary work of Twm o'r Nant has been related. The commissioning of one of these portraits by William Madocks[29] suggested the crucial role in this interaction of an urban middle-class, partly expatriate, which was also marginal to the two available critiques, although fundamental to the change in the structure of Welsh society in the modern period. This particular example, and many others, suggested that the appropriate first approach to the revaluation and location of visual images in the Welsh culture complex should be based on iconography rather than on the oeuvres of individual artists who, at that stage, were largely unidentified.

The exploration of the iconography of Twm o'r Nant and subsequently of other iconographies—of curiosities such as Dic Aberdaron, poets such as Talhaiarn, and preachers such as Christmas Evans—followed by consideration of these iconographies as group phenomena—the Bard, the Preacher, and so on—confirmed the existence of a wide range of interactions

[29] Founder of Porthmadog and Tremadog.

between classes of artefact which were isolated by both existing critiques and yet which were close to the mainstream of Welsh consciousness. The investigation of these iconographies, linking together disintegrated elements of visual culture, had the effect of revealing additional unknown artefacts, further echoing the American experience.[30] The devaluation of many of these artefacts by their marginalization outside the available critiques was made clear by the appalling condition which even icons as central to the Welsh consciousness as the seminal image of John Elias painted by Hugh Jones in 1839 had fallen. A significant number of these were found, often unidentified as well as damaged, in the national collections to which they had been donated. Many very important artefacts, known from written sources, had disappeared altogether. Some have been recovered; others remain lost.

It seems to me self-evident that our consciousness will be informed and enriched by the extension of the range of artefacts being brought together by this process. The critique which facilitates it considers the whole of visual culture as the appropriate resource, relating and binding together the artefacts by identifying interactions of consciousness and by formal influence. Among the interactions already demonstrated are the transfer of unique high art image into print, thence into naive copy, artisan-painted development, kitsch, and back into high art original as public sculpture. Another important interaction follows Welsh subject-matter into English high art image, back into Welsh high art and thence into popular art and kitsch. There are demonstrable interactions between literature, visual culture, and music. *The study of these interactions constructs an indigenous visual tradition which extends and informs other, previously established, aspects of the wider indigenous cultural tradition.*

The common factor which unites these elements of a visual culture seems to me to be their relevance to our particular national story. The complexity of the interactions intensifies as the images come closer to what existing tradition has defined as

[30] See Peter Lord, 'Iconograffeg Poblogaidd y Pregethwr', *Barn*, 330/1, 1990, and 'Ystyr y Llun Naif', *Barn*, 348/9, 1992.

the peculiar and central concerns of this story—Nonconformity, the language, the relationship with England, Celticism, industrialization, nationalism, and so on.

Therefore, the whole visual culture is the appropriate frame for the choice of material for the construction of an indigenous tradition, and an iconographic critique is the most—though not the only—appropriate guide, binding the choice to Welsh consciousness as a whole, insuring its relevance to the story. Whereas high art frame and critique are disintegrating in effect, suggesting that the culture is incomplete and lacking in internal coherence, the new frame and critique have an integrating effect, showing the culture to be many-faceted and coherent. This critique can lead to the gradual evolution of an *aesthetics based on relevance* which may, in time, sort, modify and assess the material within the national frame, establishing valued qualities and hierarchies as a basis of internal debate. This debate will not only discredit the myth of the visual handicap, but also inform the living culture through the making of new images. The establishment of this continuum from past into present by relevant aesthetics is crucial if Wales is to be anything other than living archaeology in a region of England.

The Aesthetics of Relevance is not an aesthetics of style. An object is not assessed according to its position in the story of the evolution of western art but by its position in the story of the evolution of Welsh consciousness. The concept of relevance is an extension of aesthetics, not a denial of it. It does not reduce the individual image to historical illustration but, on the contrary, demonstrates the role of the image in the historical process. In the same way, it does not deny the relative concept of quality, but requires that our comparisons are between objects which have a commonality which renders the comparison worthwhile.

The Aesthetics of Relevance does deny that the experience of high art is uniquely elevating, profound and significant. Nevertheless, it in no way rejects the product of high art culture, simply the projection of the values of that culture as absolute and universal. High art culture, in the form for instance of Welsh aristocratic patronage, is an important component in the Welsh culture complex. The Aesthetics of Relevance reassesses its meaning, and considers also the meaning of the ideology which lies behind it, in the context of the national story.

d. TWO ILLUSTRATIONS– HUGH HUGHES AND DAVID COX

i.

To activate a tradition of visual culture in Wales as a part of the mainstream of national consciousness requires the application of the new aesthetics within the education system from school to art college and university level, in the patronage system including the Arts Council and other public funding bodies and the private galleries, and in public debate generated by magazines, radio and television. Despite the general indifference within Wales to the National Museum, it remains crucial to effecting change, through its implicit status and authority as a national institution. Its policies at this time are of particular importance for two reasons. Firstly, the climate outside is changing, both in terms of available historical critique and the increasing number of indigenous young practitioners with a commitment to the particularity of Wales. Secondly, the expenditure of £24 million on new and rebuilt galleries *will enshrine the Aesthetics presented there as authoritative.*

ii.

This has been essentially a theoretical essay and not, therefore, the place to demonstrate in detail how the Aesthetics of Relevance can elucidate its raw material. Nevertheless, two small examples may help to show how far the National Museum is from aesthetics appropriate to the positive and creative interpretation of the culture it is supposed to serve.

In the Spring of 1991 the first large-scale exhibition of visual culture revealed by the new critique reached Cardiff. This exhibition, entitled 'Hugh Hughes, Artisan Painter', was intended to open the debate about the effects of high art critique in obscuring indigenous visual culture.[31] Hugh Hughes was dismissed in Rowan's *Art in Wales* in half of one sentence, but the

[31] The exhibition was organised by the National Library and also toured to Bodelwyddan Castle and the Glynn Vivian Gallery in Swansea. See the exhibition catalogue, *Hugh Hughes, Artisan Painter*, pub. National Library of Wales, 1990.

exhibition presented him as the most important painter in Wales in the first half of the nineteenth century. The Keeper of Art at the National Museum refused to show it in the Museum itself and so it was dispatched to the small gallery at Penarth, where it was not possible to maintain the logic of the exhibition design (which is crucial in a didactic exhibition) and a number of works had to be omitted. As a consequence of the location it was visited by a tiny number of people.

The exhibition was reviewed in the National Museum's own publication *Amgueddfa*. The spring 1991 edition contained 15 pages of text of which one and a half were in Welsh. The Hugh Hughes review, entitled *'Ail Ddarganfod Artist o Bwys'* ('Rediscovery of an Important Artist') was a part of that Welsh section, located next to an article about May Fair customs and a picture of folk-dancers in costume. The review was therefore unavailable to most people, locked up in the language, and subtly associated with the living archaeology of folk-dancing at Sain Ffagan. It was effectively marginalized and given the classic bookshop category, 'Welsh interest'. The main article in this issue of *Amgueddfa* was a full-page feature on Graham Sutherland, and there was also a half-page article by the Keeper of Art about the exhibition of 'The Royal Collection of Paintings from Windsor Castle'. The main story-line in this little piece, which managed to be at once both patronising and sycophantic, was that 50,000 people—'a record for an art exhibition'—had visited the attraction: 'By a short head visitors preferred the dazzling views of Venice by Canaletto to the paintings of Royal horses, carriages and soldiers commissioned by George IV when Prince of Wales from George Stubbs. Another favourite picture with many was Landseer's intimate portrait of Princess Victoire with her pet spaniel. . . The National Museum is grateful to Her Majesty the Queen for graciously giving permission for this loan which has brought so much enjoyment to our visitors and has introduced many people to the pleasure of looking at pictures—especially the best'.

In the context of the showing of the Hugh Hughes exhibition at Penarth, the last point reveals much about the attitudes of the Keeper of the Welsh national collection and about the vital importance of the Museum as an arbiter of taste in the culture. The public expression of those attitudes through exhibitions stamped with the authority of the National Museum serves only to reinforce high art critique and the homogenization of Wales within greater England. The Museum is a potent agency for the spreading of these closely related ideas. The previous year the Museum's main exhibition had been 'The Royal Wardrobe'.

The same attitudes are manifested in the new hang of the collection in the refurbished galleries at the National Museum. In the light of recent developments a gesture in the direction of indigenous painting has been made with the hanging of two pictures by Hugh Hughes and one by William Jones. The choice of the particular works and their visual context on the wall shows that nothing has changed. They are hung in a connecting staircase gallery consisting mainly of portraits of Welsh sitters by English academic painters, filled out with small landscapes by David Cox. These landscapes seem to be there by virtue only of their size in order to maintain the prissy classicism of the hang as a whole in the new galleries. This is intended to be an experience in high art aesthetics in itself. It is rather like walking through a three-dimensional stamp album. Beyond small biographical captions there is no didactic content, the artefacts are grouped in inexplicable categories which seem variously to be of period or type (portraits, landscapes and so on). Water-colours and prints are hung apart, as if they were separate phenomena, unrelated to each other and to the rest of the visual culture. It is a selection of Timothy Stevens's 'best', reluctantly modified at the edges by the need to be seen to be doing something vaguely Welsh.

The two pictures by Hughes that have been selected are not from the period of his greatest visual distinctness in the artisan manner, but from the period of his efforts to imitate contemporary English academic portraiture. One of the two, the portrait of Thomas Beynon, is distinctly more 'correct' than the other and, significantly, it is only this one which is clearly visible where the stairs ascend towards the top row of the hang. Thus Wales is tokenly represented, but homogenised into the story of the evolution of English art style, its indigenous artisan painters projected as third-rate academics.

There is another way to contextualise these same pictures by Hughes and the adjacent fillers by Cox. The almost invisible Hughes portrait is of W.J. Rees. In 1827, the year after the portrait was painted, Rees had completed the revised text of his *Hereford Guide.* David Cox, still working at that time in Hereford, was commissioned to illustrate the book with water-colours, and Hugh Hughes was commissioned to engrave Cox's originals for the publication.[32] The works and individuals presented as unrelated in the National Museum could have been brought together in a way which made important points about interactions between Welsh painters and writers, and between Welsh and English artists, and about how an aspiring Welsh portrait-painter had to supplement his income by engraving, and so on. However, this would have required (apart from an awareness of the commission) the display of a mixture of material—oil portraits, water-colours, and a book—quite at variance with the purity of the quasi-religious aesthetic experience the gallery is designed to induce.

Throwing light on Wales through the medium of the visual culture, and throwing light on the indigenous visual culture by relating it to the lives of Welsh people, are not the concerns of the Art Department of the National Museum, but rather the projection of a homogenised British culture in a way which invites favourable comparison of the institution with conservative art institutions in England and the rest of the western world.

iv.

As I have already suggested, the work of David Cox at Betws-y-coed was an important watershed in thinking about visual culture in Wales. It facilitated the development of the important notion of the relationship of the national soul to the landscape, and also to the polarization of the patriotic response to visual culture and the entrenchment of the idea of art as English. The hanging of a number of landscapes by Cox in the new galleries reminds us that the Museum is superbly equipped to explore the issue of the landscape and Welsh national consciousness from as early as the

[32] The original water-colours have survived and could, no doubt, have been made available to the Museum by the institution which holds but does not exhibit them.

seventeenth century to the present day. The failure to do so is both a failure of aspiration and of art historical critique. The exploration of this issue would require Wales to be at the centre of the Art Department's concerns, and the demonstration of interactions between literature and visual culture and between high art and popular art as the appropriate field of study. This would involve the use of sound, the Welsh language, the display of books and manuscripts, of popular art such as postcards and kitsch, all of which are apparently anathema to the image which Timothy Stevens wishes to project.

v.

By the application of this critique and the display of this range of material the National Museum could have created a Department of Visual Culture committed not only to elucidating the cultural experience of Wales in a way which would have affirmed the particularity of the culture, but which would also have affirmed the virtue of particularity as a concept. In a world of increasingly pan-cultural categories of artefact, the point needs to be made, and not simply for the benefit of Wales, that their organization and understanding in relation to each other in the context of a distinct cultural tradition can continue to assert particularity. The concerns of Wales are also the concerns of the minority cultures of the rest of the world. The new critique does not create an introspective visual tradition but one which enables us to contribute to the assertion of culture particularity everywhere.

The great potential for the enrichment of the culture—which means the enrichment of the life of everyone who chooses to identify with it—has been rejected by the institution whose only *raison d'être* is just that enrichment. The personal tragedy of the failure of the imagination of the individuals involved is that the creation of a Department of Visual Culture based on a unique critique would in fact secure for them a much higher profile and reputation in the international museum world than the competent but mindless following where others have led decades before which is all they seem capable of. Best museum practice, even in England, has begun to reject high art critique in favour of an intergrated view of visual culture exemplified for instance by the National Portrait Gallery's 'Raj' exhibition of 1990.

I have used the hanging of works by Hugh Hughes (as representative of indigenous artisan painting) and David Cox (as representative of English painters in Wales) to suggest how a different critique could change the National Museum's Art Department. Such a change would give it an important role in the contemporary culture, leading a debate which would invigorate the work of image-makers now. Hughes and Cox, and the issues they represent, are just two examples drawn from one small room of the Museum. I have explored other examples elsewhere. In any case, the changes wrought by the Aesthetics of Relevance are not predictable and absolute, but an open-ended process which should itself be the subject of revision in the future. It is, indeed, that process of revision which indicates that the culture is alive, just as the century-old ossification of aesthetics in the national institution at present signals to the world, and to ourselves—as does Sain Ffagan in a different way—that the culture is dead.

e. THE AESTHETICS OF RELEVANCE

The Aesthetics of Relevance reconstructs known material from within the critique of contribution. For instance, the work of Wilson is reassessed. To the understanding of Wilson as the progenitor of romantic English landscape, and to his understanding as the exemplar of the values of patrician society, is added his understanding by Welsh intellectuals as a metaphor for the condition of the nation. His painting is placed as a contributor to the growth of the Welsh landscape as an icon representing the National Soul.

The Aesthetics of Relevance integrates known but isolated material. For instance, because of the particular political circumstances of Wales the nineteenth century Nonconformist preachers assumed the role of national leaders. The construction of their image as leaders was both facilitated by and reflected in the visual culture. These Nonconformist icons were the product of interactions between academic art, artisan painting, popular art and naive art, all with the literary and musical culture. The existing critiques do not recognize these interactions.

The Aesthetics of Relevance reveals unknown material. Owners of disregarded works of the indigenous tradition are reassessing their meaning and bringing them to the attention of art historians and institutions. The integration of the visual image into the valued part of the culture complex of Wales instigates this reassessment by counteracting the myth of the visual handicap. In this way Hugh Hughes's masterpiece of artisan painting, 'The family of John Evans', known only from a nineteenth-century description, was revealed, for instance.

The Aesthetics of Relevance reclaims material incorporated into other national traditions as a part of the indigenous culture of Wales. For instance, the generation of the image of the Bard, a central icon of Welsh identity, was the result of a complicated interaction of Welsh and English intellectuals and artists. Decolonialised aesthetics reveal that the role of English intellectuals in its genesis no more denies the image its place in Welsh visual culture than the involvement of Wilson in the evolution of the rural idyll could deny the landscape image its central place in English visual culture. The idea that anything touched by English hands cannot legitimately be a part of indigenous Welsh tradition is an aspect of the national lack of self-confidence to which the myth of the visual handicap has contributed substantially.

The Aesthetics of Relevance re-assesses the prevalent evaluation of visual culture in the rest of the world. For instance, it might be realised that the works of late nineteenth-century Finnish nationalist artists, such as Gallen-Kallela, speak to us with more meaning than Poussin because of the parallels between their experience of the world and that of contemporary Welsh patriots. If Wales has a range of views of itself which are particular, then it must also have a range of views of the world which have particular characteristics. Wales is incomplete without its own range of world views, which must extend to visual culture as they extend to politics.